THE UNTAMED ANTHOLOGY

Books 1 - 3

BOX SET

NIGEL EDWARDS

Contents

Tame	1
Also By Nigel Edwards…	3
UNTAMED - VOL 1	5
UNTAMED - VOL 2	123
UNTAMED - VOL 3	225

"Tame:

adjective, **tam er, tam est.**

Changed from the wild or savage state; domesticated.

Tractable, docile, or submissive, as a person or the disposition.

Lacking in excitement; dull; insipid.

Spiritless or pusillanimous.

Not to be taken very seriously; without real power or importance; serviceable but harmless.

verb (used with object), **tamed, tam ing.**

to make tame; domesticate; make tractable.

to deprive of courage, ardor, or zest."

Also By Nigel Edwards...

Untamed Series...

Vol 1 - The Taming of Cambridge

Vol 2 - An Untamed Mind

Vol 3 - An Untamed Heart

Featured in...

Platonic - Eternal Love

(Poetry Anthology)

Book 1 in The Untamed Series

The Fatman Collection

Fatman Introduction

This all started when I was homeless. I stayed in a homeless project in various churches and a synagogue. The volunteers there kept on telling everyone to keep tame. I was a bit odd and annoying.

I then moved into a shared house and I told one of the guys I lived with about it. He went around telling everyone on the street that I wasn't tame. He also told them I couldn't read or write.

People on the street kept taking the piss out of me, and so I decided to write this collection of poems taking the piss out of him.

Backward

The way you do it is just no good,
You are backward.
I can't relate,
You can't even communicate.

What the hell is wrong with you?
You don't have a clue.
Every word you say,
Makes me not want to stay.

It's not how it should be,
You're nothing but a future bad memory.

Bat Shit Crazy

Stupid and lazy.
When he talks about me,
I wonder if he understands reality.
Just don't know what to say,
It's the same everyday.

Talks to me like I'm an animal,
That stupid fool.
He has no respect for anyone,
It's just not cool.

He just sits there all day,
With only negative stuff to say.
Such an unimportant man,
I say be normal, you can.

But he's bat shit crazy,
Hates everything can see.
Don't want him anywhere near me.

Been Telling Lies

Can he read and write?
Does he want a fight?
Just can't figure him out.
Want to knock him down for the count.
He keeps on lying,
I'll wait until he's crying.
What was the reason why?
Don't even try.

Cold Blooded

Like a reptile,
Never seen him smile.
Watching telly all day,
Watching time tick away.

That man is cold-blooded,
He hopes that no-one knows what he did.
Never met such a stupid man,
Whatever he says won't give a damn.

Every time he talks,
I want to walk.
Always lies,
And silly alibis.

He has no human emotion,
The way he thinks is just so slow.

Couch Potato

Might be something good on T.V tonight,
I have no life,
Don't even have a wife.
I wish I had a life.

Just sitting here all day,
Can't even get any of them hey.
Trying to think of something to say,
It always seems like the same day.

Got no friends with whom to play,
The T.V's my friend,
Come what may.

Fat and Stupid x

He is so fat and stupid,
Need to tell people what he did.
Doesn't know how to keep his mouth shut,
Sounds like he lives in a hut.

All he does is lie.
Want to belt him, would if I try.
Hate that man,
Want to get rid of him, anyway I can.

Fat, Lazy & Crazy

Had enough of that man,
Wish I could hit him,
And I can.

He doesn't listen to a fucking word,
There is nothing he has learned.

He keeps on telling lies,
Want to hit him until he cries.

Got No-One To Watch T.V With

When I get out of bed, inside I feel dead.
About my day, can't think of a word to say.
Looking out the window, there's no one I know.
Every day the same, got nothing to do again.

Haven't even got a friend, sometimes I wish this life to end.
All day in front of the T.V, nobody with me.
Can have pie and chips, don't know how to get my kicks.
This is not the life I want to live.

He Just Won't Learn

Won't listen to a word I say.
Don't want him to stay.

Want to tear his spine out.
Just won't lean,
Won't leave me alone.

Going to tear his heart out.
Get the fuck out.

Little Boy

He keeps on calling me a little boy.
Thinks he's playing with a toy.

Going to lose my temper,
Every word I can remember.

Want to teat him apart,
Going to start,
He doesn't even have a heart.

Mr. Nobody

Some people are sad,
Some people are mad.
What to say abut that twat,
He is all of that.

Everyday saying the same thing,
Over and over again.
Is there nothing in your brain?

Just sitting in your room,
No job, no wife, no life.
What do you see when you look in the mirror?
Don't you want to be who you are?

Now that you're old,
Inside you're cold.
You never went far,
Nobody cares who you are.

Self Esteem

Sitting around,
Bored out of my brains.
It's always the same,
I'm going insane.

Looking out of the window,
They are people I don't know.
Don't know where to go,
What to do, I just don't know.

If I was big and strong,
And felt like I could belong.
Can't shake this sadness out of my head,
Nobody would care if I was dead.

Don't know what to do.
People treat me like I don't have a clue.

Sofa Spud

Every day the same,
Nobody knows my name.
Wish I was somebody,
Nobody wants to know me.

Can't even get a girl,
My life is hell.
I just get fatter and fatter,
I just don't matter.

I keep on going nowhere,
No-one will care.
I'm just a fat stupid couch potato,
No-one will want to know.

Stupid Fat Man

Sick of this shit,
That stupid fat old git.
Want to jump all over his head,
I wish he was dead.
Just won't leave me alone.
Wish we didn't live in the same home.

Stupid Man

Fat, stupid man,
Will try to communicate if I can.

He just sits there and watches T.V,
As stupid as can be.

Don't want him to be with me.
He won't leave me be,

Is not all what you can see.
Want to belt him in the head,
Wish he was dead.

Not very clever,

Every word I can remember.
Just one more thing I want to say,
Shouldn't be this way.

T.V All Day

Such a useless lump of dead weight,
Full of hate.
He does nothing but sit there all day,
With nothing to say.
A man without a wife,
A man without a life.
Just couldn't live that way,
Watching T.V all day.
When I listen to his stupid words,
that man doesn't understand the bees and the birds.
Just sitting in his chair all day,
How could anyone live their life that way?

Telly

Watching T.V all day,
Making the eyes strain,
Everyday always the same.

Can think about some food to eat,
But there are no people I will meet.
Seen this film before,
I'll just sit here and watch some more.

Get up and go to bed,
Inside I feel dead.
Some sport on telly might cheer me up,
I wish I had someone to love.

Just sitting here all day,

And I'll do the same again.
No highlight to my day,
Always the same.

Might go to the shop,
Then back home.
This is where I stop,
Feeling so alone.

People ask what I've been doing,
I say not a lot.

Just going to sit here until my dying day,
I've never got anything interesting to say.

Weirdo

"Will not leave it be," is what he said to me.
Making me feel sick inside, every word a lie.
Can't understand, won't toy.
Why do what you do?
Will you listen to a word?
What have you learned?
One more time, don't lie, are you high?

Won't Learn

Won't learn,
Did try to explain,
Are you insane?

Don't know what to say,
Don't want you to stay.

Will listen to every word you say,
Not going to play.

Can't you feel my heart?
It will tear you apart.

Why won't you stop?
You don't know a lot.

They always say go with your gut,
If it was up to me he wouldn't have you shot.

Won't Leave Me Alone

Feeling sad inside,
People know I have lied.
Trying to hide.
What will they do,
When they know I have lied.

Just wanted some company,
But nobody wants to be with me.
Just don't want them to ignore,
Don't know what I do this for.

All I ever get is, "leave me alone",
And no-one ever calls on the phone.

Stupid Words

His stupid words echo around my head.
I hate every word he said.
Sitting there,
Letting everyone know he don't care.

There must be something I can do,
But he just doesn't have a clue.
Always telling lies and eating too many pies.
Nothing in his life but T.V
Do not want this man with me.

But the creep won't leave me alone,
Wish we didn't live in the same home.
That cheap, lousy, scumbag lives in a dream world.

It makes me sad there are people like that.
To hell with the twat."

Backwards II

Barking mad,
Sad and just bad.
As backwards as you like,
Can't read or write.

I don't do a thing but watch T.V,
Nobody wants to be with me.
When I look in the mirror,
I don't like what I see.

I'm ugly as can be.
There is nothing I like about me.
I don't understand what people say.
Want to enjoy life, but just can't find a way.

The Untamed Collection

As I explained in the introduction to the Fat Man collection, this taming thing was a bit weird. What happened next was sick. People decided that some of them are untame. Things got really insane. The untame people got beaten up and everybody treated them like shit.

I don't know what happened but it got really crazy.

Cheap and Tacky

Cheap and tacky,
This taming is so wacky.
The people of Cambridge,
Don't even understand the language

In mt home town,
People need to slow down.
As I walk around,
What they say is just stupid sound.

The vile words they spew out of their mouths,
They are like sick and disturbed animals.
They keep asking who I have hit.
This taming is bullshit.

Taming

Telling me I need taming
Is an odd way of complaining.
Can't tell if they are putting it on,
Not sure where they are coming from.

Things have got so crazy,
Do these people really hate me?
Shouldn't paint people with the same brush,
But they treat me like I don't mean much.

How can this be?
Are all the untamed the same as me?
What they say is not true,
Don't they have a clue?

There has been blood shed,
And some of them are dead.
This has gone too far,
Don't even know who these people are.

Demons

They are not humans, more like demons.
A disease has spread amongst the people,
They are turning evil.

I do try to ask questions,
But all I get is lies.
Perhaps it doesn't matter,
No one cares about why.

They can all go to hell.
I'd put them in a prison cell.
The strange order of the day,
Some tame, others untame.

I know people are not very smart,
They tame others without out any art.

It's like someone opened up pandora's box,
The demons walk the earth.
Some people don't care what life is worth.

Don't belong

They keep on saying I should be in a cell.
That would make my life a living hell.

My name doesn't matter,
I'm just one of the untamed.
I don't mind people not knowing my name,
but this is insane.

They say I can't read or write,
and I don't know how to live my life.
I don't know what I did wrong.
Always making me feel like I don't belong.

Everywhere I Go

They hate my guts,
but they don't know me,
I think they're nuts.

Here in my home town,
They all want to put me down.
Don't want to get out of bed,
They wish I was dead.

I remember years ago,
It was not so.
But the good times are gone,
Now I feel like I don't belong.

Why say I'm this way?

They should be broken,
Don't even know them.

They call me untame,
without even knowing my name.
They hate me everywhere I go.
They haven't got a clue,
What did I do?

Hell

Taming has lead to bloodshed.
People are dead.
I remember when people were normal.
Was it all in my head?

What they have been doing is awful.
It's like someone cast an evil spell,
And opened the door straight to hell.
The people have gone mad, this taming is just so sad.

You don't tame people, don't they even know?
We are told to keep tame wherever we go,
From people we don't know.

This has torn people apart.
The people are not very smart.

My Home Town

The people in my home town have gone crazy,
They keep telling me to throw in the towel.
Something has gone really wrong,
People make me feel like I don't belong.

Don't know what to say, it shouldn't be this way.
Everyday I've got to listen to the stupid stuff they say.
They never think they might be doing it the wrong way.

Now they say everyone is tame or untame,
And it doesn't matter about your name.
It's not normal, people are awful and losing the plot.

Wish this could all be forgot.

Pork Pies

Don't know if I will grow to be old.
Don't have to listen to every word I've been told.
Sometimes people just tell pork pies.
Why do people tell lies?

I remember before everyone became tame or untame,
People called me by my name.
It feels like the world has gone insane.
I hope taming never happens again.

How can people have so much hate?
So much stupidity and lack of maturity.
Some people just don't get normality.
Or even reality.

Don't know if I will grow to be old.
Don't have to listen to every word I've been told.
Sometimes people just tell pork pies.
Why do people tell lies?

I remember before everyone became tame or untame,
People called me by my name.
It feels like the world has gone insane.
I hope taming never happens again.

How can people have so much hate?
So much stupidity and lack of maturity.
Some people just don't get normality.
Or even reality.

Sick

I'm so sick of the people,
They behave like they no nothing at all.
Walking down the street,
Listening to the people I meet.

They won't grow up,
I've had enough.
Listening to their stupid words,
People never learn.

Now they have decided everyone is tame and untame,
It's so insane.
I'm so sick of these stupid people,
They are so evil.

They act as if life is a T.V show,
And they're making a cameo.
They're so fake I have to remind myself,
They're actually awake.

I wish they would be swallowed up in a giant earthquake.

Can't See

Blinded by the lies,
I have no idea what you see with your eyes.
You can't see a thing,
You don't know me.

How did this madness spread?
How many people need to be dead?
Can't see the reason why,
This is all one big lie.

Back before they thought I was untamed,
People would address me by my name.
What the hell is wrong with these people?
Why are they now so evil?

Just one more thing to say,
It should not be this way.

Stupid People

The people of Cambridge are the stupidest people in the world.

World famous for their uni,
They have all gone loony.
It's just so insane,
Nowadays everyone is tame or untame,
It's lame.

Don't these people have brains?
How an there be tame and untamed?
I know some people have low IQs.
The people of Cambridge don't have a clue.

The Untamed

People don't care abut my name,
They just call me untame.
People keep acting insane,
They all hate me now I'm untame.

They ask me who have I hit.
It's not something I do, I don't get it.
They say I should be in a cell,
I try to ask why, but they do not tell.

They want to make me cry,
I don't know why.
They are going to kick my head in,
There is no way I can win.

Trying to communicate

I do try to listen to the words people say,
But not sure if they do it the other way.
Some people are just so simple,
They think words don't mean anything at all.

They keep on saying we need to keep tame,
Everyday it's the same.
I try to say I'm not a lion,
Are you having me on?

Some of these people are just so sick,
And intellectually weak.
Trying to communicate can be impossible,
Some people say do you want a ball?

Could put in a ponytail,
It's just as stupid as hell.
Man is not tame or untame,
It is just so lame.

Trying

Don't know how to explain,
We are not all the same.
Won't you listen to a word I say,
Isn't there anything you have learned?

I am trying to explain that I don't feel the same.
Why do I try?
It's enough to make me cry.
I won't tell you a lie.
I don't understand why I ever try.

Untame Man

Everywhere I go people say I will go on the run,
They're all so dumb.
They call me a violent criminal,
Treating me like I'm nothing at all.

Everyone treats me like a fool,
They want me to fail.
They laugh at me and say I can't read or write,
It's a bit more than just impolite.

As they pass me by,
Asking if I cry,
None of this is true,
They just don't have a clue.

I'm nothing but an untamed man,
Is this some satanic plan?
Who are the other untame men?
This needs to end, and never be done again.

What is Wrong with the People?

People have been trying to break my heart,
What they have been saying,
Is I'm not very smart.

As I walk down the street,
It's the same with everyone I meet.
They think I'm someone I'm not,
They treat me like I don't mean a lot.

What the hell is wrong with people?
They just say I'm untame,
And us untamed are all the same.

What does it even mean?

Hasn't anyone got a clue?
Don't know what to do.

Will Never Forgive

Something has poisoned the brains,
There are no tames and untames.
People need to wash that poison,
Out of their brains.

It is like they are in an hypnotic trance,
I try to reason but I have no chance.
A dark cloud has been cast over Cambridge,
They use a primitive language.

They have been doing it for far too long,
How can this happen in the town where I'm from?
I will never forgive,
These people don't deserve to live.

Dirty Old Man Collection

The problems with the guy I was living with were never ending. Problems with people on the street continued so I moved to a different house, hoping these problems would come to an end, but the problems got worse.

I moved in with two dirty old men. One called Mello Yello, and the other I nicknamed the Goblin.

They did the same thing, they told everyone around I hit people and I couldn't read or write, and I was untame.

Things just got more and more crazy.

Deplorable

He doesn't want people to know,
Hasn't got anywhere to go.
Doesn't do a thing,
Wishes he could be unseen.

Just watches T.V all day,
Doesn't want people to know he's gay.
Sits there like a useless lump of dead weight,
Full of hate.

Deplorable and unemployable.

Says everyone needs to learn to be tame,
Does this everyday.

Such a sad lonely old man,
Has no life, has no plan.

Dirty Old Man

Just sitting there all day,
Got nothing to say.
Just sat in front of the T.V,
A man no-one wants to see.
Got nothing to look forward to,
Got nothing to do.
Pisses off everyone around,
Never has his feet on the ground.
Lives in a fantasy world,
Tells everyone won't do what he's told.

He tries to be bold, but inside he's cold.

Evil Elf

That stupid little evil elf,
Acts like he is twelve.
Not a proper man,
So small he could fit in a can.
Creeps around like a bug on the ground.
Has sickness inside his head,
No-one will care when he's dead.

Evil Goblin

The old man reminds me of an evil goblin,
The sort of man who will never win.
Like some mythical monster, he won't go far.
Crying his eyeballs out, will go to hell no doubt.

Sits in front of the T.V all day, want to push him out of the way.
That man is sick in the head, wish he was dead.

Evil

The ungodly little goblin will never win.
This way he has lived his life is a sin.
Don't know where to begin, such a stupid evil goblin.
I hope he burns in hell.
You should be in a cell.

Fiend

When I look into his eyes,
I don't know why he tells so many lies.
The man is a fiend,
He's not what I need.
He has sickness in his soul,
I want to bury him in a hole.
He makes me want to puke my guts up,
Doesn't understand love.
They should put him back in his cell,
Then send him straight to hell.

III
―――

That old man has got a sickness inside his head,
Wish he was dead.
Just sits there all day,
Won't listen to what I say.
Should be in a cell,
Hope you go to hell.
Stupid sick old man,
As ill as the son of Sam.

In a prison cell

That stupid little gremlin,
Want to tear him limb from limb.

Don't want to remember him,
My patience is running thin.

Can't hit him, feeble little goblin.
Just sits there with his pot belly, watching telly.

Really hope he burns in hell,
Should be in a prison cell.

Mello Yello

A man known by may names,
A man with no brains.

They call him Mello Yello,
Not a man I want to know.

The kids call him the evil one,
Just as stupid no-one.

They should never have let him out of his prison cell.
Hope people give him hell.

The weirdest weirdo I have ever met in my life.
With him it is always trouble and strife.

Sad, Mad, and Bad

Sitting on his own,
No-one calling on the phone.
Got no friends to play with,
Got no love to give.

One of life's losses,
So sad and useless.
Have to listen to his stupid words everyday,
Even though he's got nothing to say.

Scared of his own shadow,
Stupid, fat and shallow.
Inside he is hollow,
Not someone I want to know.

Sick and Loathsome

Just sitting there watching your life waste way,
With nothing to say.
Just watching T.V all day everyday,
Can't give any of them hey.
Got demons inside your head,
It's like you're already dead.
Such a sick and loathsome man,
No-one will be a fan.
So fat and lazy, stupid, old and crazy.

Stupid

As stupid as a man can be,
Lives in a fantasy.
Just sits there all day watching T.V,
Do not want him to be with me.

Such a stupid liar,
Want to set him on fire.
Just a stupid old perv,
Don't know where he gets the nerve.

Aways trying to cause problems,
It never ends.
The world is better of without people like him,
The sort who will never win.

Silly Weirdo

He sits there in his dream world,
Inside he is cold.
Such a sad silly weirdo,
Not someone I want to know.

Keep on saying people need taming,
It's all need to be tame, so lame.
Can't even read a book,
Doesn't have a good look.

The world's most boring man,
If I say it is black,
He will say it's white,
Doesn't even have a life.

Can't get a job,
Always on his tod.

T.V Everyday

Don't understand how someone can watch T.V all day everyday.
The old man just sits there moaning about this and that.

How can you live your life that way,
Just sitting there everyday?
No-one ever wants him around,
For him no love can be found.

Don't want him in my life,
He should be in a cell,
I hope he goes to hell.

The Evil Little Goblin

The ungodly little goblin will never win.
The way he has lived his life is a sin.
Don't know where to begin, such a stupid evil goblin.
Hope you burn in hell, you should be in a cell.

The Evil One

The kids call him the evil one,
Just a stupid no-one.
Wants to be a mob boss,
Whatever he does it will be a loss.

Watching T.V all day,
Wasting away.

He makes me want to throw my guts up,
I've had enough.
He is a man no-one will love,
Won't end up in heaven above.

The Grim Goblin

Looks like he lives in a rubbish bin,
    The dirty old grim goblin.
    One of them dirty old men,
    I hope never to see him again.

Just watches T.V all day,
    How can a man live his life that way?
    A real life boogyman,
    Should have kept him in the can.

A Wasted Life

FUNERAL POEM

Mello Yello
The worst weirdo I have ever met in my life.

Once there was a man,
I don't want to remember him,
But I can.

While he walked on this earth,
He never knew what he was worth.
Dumb as a bag of rocks,
I hate him lots.

Criminal scum,
Didn't know how to have fun.

Just T.V all day everyday.
Never got a job, never meant a lot.

The sickest, most disgusting, perverted moron it has been my displeasure to ever meet.

The Taming Of Cambridge

Taming continues. Different things can effect different groups of people. Mass hysteria, mind control, old mentality. Not sure how to explain it. This has caused a lot of harm, but I am sure it is some sort of sickness.

There is no logic. People keep floating around like they do everything on autopilot. One thing I noticed is they don't do it to rich people. It has been a long time since things have been normal.

Cloven Hoof

People treat me as if I walk around with a cloven hoof.
What they say is not the truth.
They always say who have I hit.
They sound like they mean it.

Telling me I'm going to be tamed,
Is insane.
Such a stupid use of language,
What is wrong with the people of Cambridge?

Crazy

The people of Cambridge have gone crazy,
They don't even understand why they do this to me.
When I was growing up taming was what you did to lions,
Don't know where they get their lies from.

They treat all of the untame people as if they are the same person,
Where are these people coming from?
They take the piss and do all they can to hurt,
Then walk off saying, "why can't we just get on?"

People have had their heads kicked in,
They act like it doesn't mean a thing.

This is just so insane, they don't even know my name.
And tomorrow they will do it again.

Every Day is the Same

Walking around, we communicate with sound.
What they say is the same everyday,
Again, again and again is driving me insane.
Now that my name is untame.

They say I should be in a cell, they can all go to hell.
Some people only get off and on, do you get where I'm coming from?
I try to ask them why they think I'm untame,
But they don't even want to know my name.

Everyday

Have we got to do this again?
It's always the same.
Nowadays they call me vulnerable tame,
They have all gone insane.

They harass,
And are so crass.
The people of Cambridge,
Don't seem to understand language.

They seem like they are in a hypnotic trance,
I get no answers to the questions I ask.
Hope they all go to hell,
This is making me feel unwell.

Mass Hysteria

Cambridge is suffering from mass hysteria,
Effecting everyone in the area.
People have gone insane, they talk about me,
But don't know my name.

They say I can't read or write,
Pretend they want to fight.

None of this makes any sense,
Need some sort of psychological self-defence.
They call it taming,
This needs explaining.

People Are So Fake

Walking around in a day dream,
With your head in a cloud.
Not sure if you care about the words you say,
This is not all play.

Can't believe how simple you are,
You won't go far.
You said some people are tame,
And others untame.

Don't even want to know your name,
We are not the same.
You don't even know how to communicate,
You are so fake.

As soft as a snowflake.

People Should Keep Tame

Trying to enjoy my walk,
Don't want to listen to others talk.
Taming is not funny,
Talking to me like I'm a puppy.

They teach it in church,
They teach it in school,
Talking to me,
Like I'm a fool.

Don't they have a clue?
This is not what people should do.
Asking me who I have hit,
Do some of them mean it?

Saying that I can't read or write,
They're the ones who aren't too bright.

Stupid Madness

The taming is pathetic sadness.
It's stupid madness.
The people of Cambridge used to be normal,
Now they are just bloody awful.

They don't know how to wash the poison out of their brains,
They have gone insane.
They have started calling people vulnerable tames,
They do this without knowing their names.

Too many people have been hit,
This is stupid bullshit.
Why can't they understand this is wrong?
They're too far gone.

The Taming of Cambridge

I can remember the words people said, not very clever.
They are trying to make me out to be someone I'm not,
And treat me like I don't mean a lot.

Everywhere I go, they talk to me like I'm someone they know.
What the hell have they been doing?
How many people got beaten up?
Can't people feel love?

They never listen to a thing I say.
The same stupid shit everyday.

Have they all gone crazy?
They are so intellectually lazy.

I call it the taming of Cambridge,
We are tame or untame, this is insane.

It's Called Taming

It's called taming.
And this needs some explaining.
That's what people say.
Everyday.

Just some silly baby talk.
Not going to stay, I'll take a walk.
This has sent some to the grave.
People just don't know how to behave.

The people of Cambridge,
Need to learn language.
Too many people have been hit,
This is stupid shit.

It needs to stop, it needs to end.
I don't want it to happen to a friend.

Cambridge

The people of Cambridge,
Are the dirtiest scum you can imagine,
Don't know where to begin.
They have people tamed,
This needs to be explained.

They don't even think,
This goes on week after week,
Month after month,
Year after year.

It's been going on for so long now,
In my home town.
People are not tame or untame,
Have they all gone insane?

Won't Leave me Be

What can I do?
You don't have a clue.
What can I say?
It shouldn't be this way.

What's the reason why?
All you do is lie.
Don't want to lose my temper,
About what you can't remember.

I'll ask you again,
My words can you recall them?
Why won't you leave me be?
You're nothing to do with me.

What's the point of calling me untame?
I do have a name.
You won't listen to a word.
Did you even go to school you fool?

How did it get to be this way?

I walk down the street,
Wondering who I will meet.
They all call me one of the untames,
We don't even know each other's names.

They try to make me feel like shit,
And ask me who I have hit.
They don't understand,
That's not how I want to use my hand.

But they say it anyway,
This is not play.
Then they say soon I'll be in a cell,
They are making my life hell.

I ask, why am I untame?
They just laugh and say it's my name.

Don't Belong

They keep on saying I should be in a cell,
Making my life a living hell.
My name doesn't matter,
Im just one of the untamed,
I don't mind people not knowing my name,
but this is insane.

They say I can't read or write,
I won't know how to live my life.
Don't know what I did wrong,
Want to make me feel like I don't belong.

Trying to walk

This is a systematic dumbing down of the people,
They are getting evil.
They have such a limited vocabulary,
When they talk to me.

Don't know what they can see,
Saying I won't get a key.
How can two men tell each other to keep tame,
It's just so lame.

Talking about me, saying we need to keep you tame,
You don't even know my name.
Just silly baby talk,
Just trying to walk.

Wait until you've been tamed

Something has poisoned their brains,
Everyday is the same.
They don't listen to a word I say,
And call me untame.

When an untame gets beaten up,
They show him no love.
They all say you got tamed,
This needs to be explained.

This taming is a disease,
Too much hate people please.

Cambridge is Cursed

Evil has spread like wildfire,
Everyone has become a liar.
People act like they can't hear a word,
I say it shouldn't be this way.

It's like they are in a hypnotic trance,
So many questions I want to ask.
There is no such thing as tame and untame people,
The only word I can think of is evil.

Cambridge has a curse,
How can it get any worse?

Something wrong with the people

The people in my home town,
Keep on saying I need to throw in the towel.
They have turned into disgusting animals,
They are childish fools.

They have turned some people into untame men.
They call me one of them.
Everywhere I go,
I get disrespect from people I don't know.

Something is very wrong with the people,
They keep on asking me to go out on the pull.
Always pestering me for my attention,
With another stupid question.

All the time they lie.
I don't even think they know the reason why.

We Bully

Everyday listening to the same stupid words,
    No lessons learned.
    Again and again,
    Every day the same.

They say we bully,
    People in my home town, as I walk around.
    They don't just do this to me,
    Don't know what they can see.

They treat us all as if we are the same.
    They need to learn man in not tame or untame,
    But every day is the same.

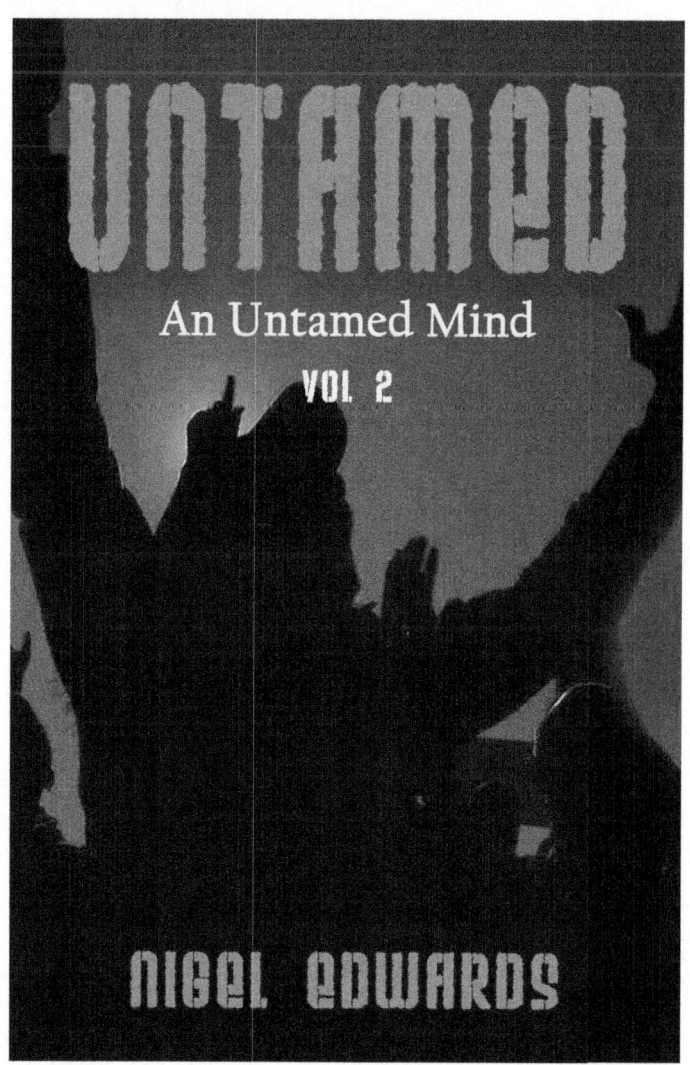

Book 2 in The Untamed Series

Part 1

NO HOPE

Tomorrow will always be the same
Tomorrow will always be the same,
This one thought rolling round my brain
Something needs to change, It's driving me insane.

People looking at me as though I'm the one to blame.
Spitting out with looks of hatred, I'm their society's stain.

Tomorrow will always be the same,
But maybe tomorrow they'll bow their heads in shame.

I'm trying to keep it together but all they show me is distain.
The fuse is lit, pressure mounting, they'll be the
Able to my Cain.

No Hope

I can hear him, shouting through the hallways. Mr. Entitled. Mr. Old and Perverted. Mr. Nothing. He's been here longer than any of the others. A halfway house he has called his own. The leg up he's chosen to ignore and instead of making plans to move on, get a place of his own, has set up camp in his shitty little dorm room.

I call him The Fat Man. An apt description for the grotesque leach on society's dwindling resources. If he was on the street he'd be dead already. A comforting thought.

I feel sorry for the staff here at this place. They're fantastic, they're here to genuinely help us, get us back on track in this world, and the Fat Man takes advantage. They can't kick him out, they can only try and nudge him in the right direction, help him look for a place he can call his own, help him manage his money so that he can start making something of his life. They do it for all of us, they are our gateway back into real life. They are there if we want to talk about what went wrong, or they will keep their distance if we need to quietly contemplate our lives. But this is a temporary existence. A means to an end. This is not anyone's forever home.

'I need my baccy. Someone go to the shop for me,' I hear the Fat Man hollar from outside of my door.

He receives no response and slams his fist into the wall.

Go yourself, you fat, lazy cretin. You're fifty-two years old not eighty-two. put one foot in front of the other and walk the two hundred yards down the road the corner shop.

'Oy, dickhead, go get me my baccy,' he cries out, slamming his fist into my door now.

The bang makes me jump in bed. An icy finger of adrenaline making its way through the pit of my stomach.

We've had words before. When I arrived here two weeks ago Fat Man zeroed in on me, goading me, wanting to turn my easygoing nature into something far more sinister. I tried ignoring him but he persisted until I needed to threaten him with violence and the staff were forced to get involved.

'We know what he's like, but violence will not be tolerated here. Keep that in mind and just ignore him.'

It's hard to do that when he's stood outside your door first thing in the morning watering his fists against it.

'Oy faggot, stop wanking in there and go get me my baccy. I'll let you have a rollie for your troubles.'

What an utterly disgusting man. Who does he think he is? The untitled inbred, strutting around the place as though he owns it, barking orders at the other guests.

Another battering at the other side of my wall springs me out of bed. I'm not having it. I yank open the door and scream at him to fuck off.

He turns into my outburst and smirks, lurching towards me.

As a natural reaction to his movements I put my hand out in defence, to stop him getting any closer. My palm connects with his oncoming chest and he falls over just as one of the staff turns onto the corridor. They couldn't have been here a moment earlier, could they? They couldn't have been witness to him moving towards me with aggression?

No, of course they couldn't.

Instead it looks like I pushed him and he fell. It looks like I am the aggressor towards this fat, elderly waste of life.

'Woah, calm it men. Get back in your room,' the staff member, John, tells me.

There is a strict no drugs, alcohol or violence policy here at this place. Understandably so. The last thing these guys need is bedlam underneath their roof. Although I have been happy to trade my alcohol abuse picked up on the street, for a warm bed to call my own, and drugs never really did it for me. As for violence? You see it from time to time when you're homeless. Others will try to rob you for anything you might have, so there is the occasional need to fight back. In here though I've been at peace. I haven't felt the need to lash out. I have had my sanctuary, my little room consisting of a single bed, small table in the corner, and cupboard to keep my things in. I haven't had to stand up for what is mine while in here because no one has really bothered me. No-one but the Fat Man. And now it looks like I attacked him.

'Did you see that? He pushed me over,' the Fat

Man tells John as the staff member leans over to help him up off the floor.

I stand in my doorway and watch with disgust.

'I didn't,' I try to voice and am met with John's palm to quiet me.

'Alright, come on, lets get you up off this floor.'

John struggles lifting the Fat Man, and playing the victim, Fat Man does little to help himself back onto his feet.

John is new here. He's been here a month or so, a little longer than me, but still, he's learning the ropes.

'Can you help with his other arm?' John asks me.

I shake my head, 'I'm not touching that,' I tell him and then step back into my room and close the door.

I go and sit down on my bed, listening to both men huffing and pushing in union. Clenching my fists together into balls of fury, I take a few deep breaths, slowly exhaling, closing my eyes to reach a place of serenity in my mind.

That man.

Most of the other guests here are fine. It is just him and his scraggy mate The Goblin who cause issues. Both of them much older, greyer and more bitter the rest of us.

I don't know what it is. I have tried to understand them, tried to have a conversation with both of them, but it is no use. They see the rest of us as young scum, drug addicts, smack-heads out for a free ride. They don't understand it is them who are the vermin and they don't care either.

I listen to John huffing and puffing, straining under the weight of helping Fat man to his feet. The noise subsides as they move off down the corridor.

I roll myself a cigarette.

There is a no smoking policy in the building which means I'll have to go outside for this, through the lounge area and past reception. People will have no doubt already heard how I "hit" Fat Man. Lies and misunderstandings travel fast around here.

Lying back on my bed I close my eyes, recalling the other life I lived not so long ago, and how things can slip so damn quickly.

I had the flat, the girlfriend, the job which came with work mates who turned into friends. I was a warehouse worker, a picker and packer who moved up to supervisor after a couple of years. Admittedly, it wasn't the best job in the world, but it wasn't the worst either and it paid decent enough, there was always overtime available to top up the wage.

I met her in a pub one night. Me and the lads would always go for a couple of drinks after work. We worked the 6am-6pm shift, four days on, four days off but, like I said, could come in on day five for a half day at double time.

This particular evening we had moved on from the first pub. It was about nine o'clock on a Saturday night and I'd just finished my fifty four hour week and been paid the previous day.

There she was, stood at the end of the bar with her mate. A tiny little thing. I think the word is petite. Straight dark hair and the bluest eyes I'd ever seen. She smiled when I smiled at her. I offered to buy her and her mate a drink and that was it, those two ladies merged into our group.

I don't want to mention her name. The very thought of it still conjures up feelings of anger, sadness, rage and love…of course love. Because I loved her so much and I thought she loved me.

Lets call her The Heart Breaker.

The drinks were flowing, we were all laughing and joking. Slowly some of the other lads started to flake out or receive phone calls from their other halves summoning them home. The old curly finger.

And then it was just me, one of the younger lads who I worked with, Heart Breaker, and her mate.

The girls wanted to move on to a club to dance and we readily agreed. At some point I found myself dancing with Heart Breaker, and then kissing her, and then in a taxi to my flat with her, and then in bed with her.

Smiling, I recall her words after the sex.

"I'm not just some slag who shags about. If I share my body with you I want to start sharing my life.'

It was a little full on, granted, but I liked that. She wasn't afraid to say how she felt. There were no mind games, just what appeared as complete honesty.

And so I fell in love and she moved in.

Things were great. Really, really great. We laughed, we loved, we took the piss out of each other, we walked hand in hand through the park on lazy Sunday afternoons, we fucked like rabbits. We were sickeningly happy, like a regular fairytale couple in their honeymoon period. I'd get butterflies in my stomach every time I'd see her. We made plans for our future together, we were going to go on holiday, see the world, maybe one day have children. She became my everything and then she tore my heart right out of my chest by cheating on me.

I fell hard for her and when she was gone I started drinking. Heavy. My mornings would consist of a half bottle of vodka to blow away the cobwebs, and I'd then head off to the pub, where I'd stay until closing time. Having people around me helped. I felt like I was getting over it, moving on, but really I was spiralling down into oblivion.

After enough days passed where I rang in sick for work, I was eventually invited in for a performance review. I was drunk for that interview and my boss knew it. He didn't say anything but I knew he knew. I was demoted. My supervisor position stripped from me, and I was back on picking.

Not long after I was told they would "sadly" have to let me go. I didn't care. I hadn't been in work much for past few months anyway. My new friends at the pub I drank in didn't work. They were living the dream. They had money coming in from government benefits. Beer tokens they called them. I became one of them. I applied for my beer tokens and drank myself into oblivion until one day I came home to find an eviction notice in the post.

Funny thing receiving state handouts. It turns

out they aren't just beer tokens after all. That money is means tested as the very minimum of what people need to live on. You're supposed to pay your rent, your gas, electric, water, council tax, buy in food, and then there isn't really anything left to use as beer tokens. If you spend it all on beer then you can't pay your bills and if you can't pay your bills you get evicted and end up homeless.

It's a strange feeling stepping out onto the street and having nowhere to go, your possessions reduced to a what fits into a backpack. No plan, no direction, no money, no food, no hope.

The first few days friends from the pub offered out their couches for me to crash on but it didn't take long for them to ask me to move on. They couldn't afford to feed me with their beer tokens. Not after paying their bills and being left with what they were left with.

You don't notice it when you're a contributing member of society, you are blind to the underbelly of the streets. There are far more homeless than you'd ever expect to see.

Walking aimlessly around that first night, my eyes were opened to the harsh realities of the street. The underbelly are generally friendly, each one of us has their own story of how they landed here. It is a soulless existence, having nowhere to go, nothing to do, scavenging for scraps, morsels of pity from those who live with direction.

I lived this way for 92 days. Fortunately it was through the summer months. Then I got a place here and I'm determined never to end up back there. My life was on track before I met the Heart Breaker. I was somebody and then I became a ghost. My life goals are somewhat different to those of the man I once was, mt hopes and dreams humbled after hitting rock bottom and still falling.

A knock at my door.

I jump up from the bed and open the door. It's Clive, the site's supervisor, a good guy who seems to genuinely want to help people find there feet.

'Hi pal, can we have a chat?'

I smile and nod, following him out of my room and down the corridor to his office close to reception.

'This about the Fat man?' I ask and catch Clive's smirk.

'He does have a name you know?'

"And so do I. One that isn't Dick head or Faggot, or Smack head.'

Another nod from Clive as we enter his office and he invites me to take a seat.

'So, there's been a allegation made that you pushed him over. John came around the corner moments too late so didn't witness the altercation. What's your version of events?'

I scoff at this.

'Fat Man is a bully. He's a piece of shit who preys on those he perceives as weak. I'm not weak and I didn't push him over, he came at me, I put my hand up to stop him and he fell, landing on his fat arse.'

A nod.

A note written on a piece of paper in front of him.

'Anything else?'

'Yes, you need to keep an eye on that guy. He's constantly goading not just me, but others at this site. I've got bigger concerns and I want this place to be a stepping stone back into society, but men like him will try and beat you down. It only takes one of them to snap, fight back and they're then thrown out of this place because of him.'

'Can't you all just get along?' Clive asks, and I feel the frown forming on my brow.

'How? He's scum. If he wasn't here he'd be

dead on the street by now. There is just no talking to some people, trying to make them understand is pointless. Scum.'

Another nod.

'And how are you getting on here?'

'I'm good. Trying to ignore the arseholes, keeping myself to myself, writing poetry as a way for venting instead of lashing out.'

'That's good. That's great actually. What's the poetry about?'

I smile. 'Life, this place, attitudes, society…'

'And the Fat Man?' Clive asks with a grin.

'Oh yeah, he's the star of the show in some of the poems.'

I'm so disgusted

I'm so disgusted with the people of Cambridge,
Taming is a load of rubbish.
Never heard so much stupid bullshit,
They just keep on doing it.

To begin with I thought it would fade away,
But they just kept on doing it everyday.
They make it difficult to ignore what they say,
But it's the same stupid shit everyday.

Want me to agree to be tame?
Really it's talking the wrong way.
It's just so odd explaining this to normal people,
The way they talk is so simple.

If your untame you can't read or write,
And your not very bright.

You're someone who hits people,
So they beat you up and treat you like shit,
And never stop doing it.

Bone-Head

Less than the fingers I have on one hand,
Less seconds than that.
Quicker than you can blink your eyes,
Why do you keep telling lies?
Trying too hard, you better be on guard.

Broken down

Hated by everyone around,
Trying not to be found.
All day everyday in front of the T.V.
I want him to stay away from me.

Just a broken down dirty old man,
Will get rid of him as soon as I can.
He always makes me feel sick,
And his body is weak.

Hope there is a special place in hell,
And while on earth should be in a cell.

Cambridge Has Gone Insane

Had it up to the eyeballs, with silly fools.
These stupid pointless pissy little people.
Can't tell if they are putting it on,
But taming is very wrong.

Why have people been hitting you?
These people just don't have a clue.
It's not something they should do.

We are destroying your heart,
Won't feel any loss when we are apart.
You have no way of moving forward,
These people are no good.

This has been going on for so long,

They never think that it is wrong.
Why won't you leave me be?
Why do they even want to talk to me?

We need to keep you tame, Cambridge has gone insane.

Can't Do Anything Technical

Can't do anything technical,
Are you trying to be cool?
Really I think you sound like a fool,
Talking to me like I'm a tool.

Are you kidding, I went to school,
Then it's when I go out on the pull.
Can't I just be on my own?
Want to go home.

But they do it again, do they want me to hate them?
Calling me untame again, and again.

Fantasy

Some people live in a fantasy world,
The evil one and the ugly goblin,
The sort that like to go out robbing.

Dark and cold inside, them dirty old men, nobody will like them.
So hateful and disgraceful.

Wish they were dead,
Won't even leave me alone,
Even when I'm in bed.
Even when I'm in the shower,
The evil one thinks he's in power.

People need to know they treat me like a Neanderthal.
They just keep on saying I can't read or write,
As if I was born last night.

Can't wait to be rid of them, those sick old men.
They don't get reality, keep lying about me.

Keep saying I hit people,
And I'm evil.
Such stupid little people.

They keep on losing their temper,
And act like I can't remember.
Then go around telling people I'm untame,
Everyday is the same.

Keep on causing me problems with people, they are truly evil.
Need to say it again, man is not tame or untame.

Don't know why some people are this way,
Just sitting there watching TV all day.
They are the scum of the earth,
Don't even know what human life is worth.

Should throw them back in their cells, and when they die they will go to hell.

Fuck The Score

The house always wins,
The story finishes then begins.
Sharks swimming with their fins,
My feet feel like they're walking on pins.

I hate their stupid grins,
Who always wins?
Don't know how to take it,
Why would you break it?

Have People Been Hitting You?

Walking down the street,
Wondering who I will meet.
They don't even know my name,
But I have to explain, again.
People are not tame and untame.

Looking at their stupid eyes,
They keep telling lies.

They ask again and again.
Have people been hitting you?
No they didn't do.
These people don't have a clue.

You poor little thing,
He can't even read or write.

Got No Way Of Moving Forward

Listening to people speak,
They sound so intellectually weak.
Keep on saying I can't do anything technical,
What a load of bull.

This has been going on for years,
Not going to say cheers.

Then they say I've got no way of moving forward,
It makes me feel awkward.
They walk past and say,
'I'm untame,' and do it again.

How Could They Do It?

How could they support taming,
This isn't computer gaming.
Taming is harassment and abuse,
It does not amuse.

They just show up and say,
Who is untame?
Don't want to take the piss,
But how could they do this?

They should be against taming,
The law is what they are breaking.

I Am The One They Will Hate

I am the one they are laughing at,
Treating me like a prat.
It's not like I say,
I'll do it when you are in the way.

Then it's what are you barking at,
Like I threatened them with a bat.

I need to explain again,
People are not tame or untame.
They know not what they do,
Don't have a clue.

If You Treat People Like Animals

If you treat people like animals,
If you talk to people like they are animals.
I do try to explain this taming is insane.

They think the solution is people need to keep tame,
Do they even think about what they say?

Looking into my eyes,
Keep telling me lies.
They teach it in church, they it in schools.
Are all the people fools?

You can tame a cat,
Stop talking to me like a twat.

Numbskull

Bonehead,
You're gonna be dead.
You heard what I said.
You can't get that girl in bed.
Your gonna be dead.
What do you think about,
When you're in bed?
Do you listen to a word anyone said?

People Are Making Me Feel Ill

They say whatever I do I will fail,
The script is stale.
Do they think it's a pantomime?
What they're doing is a crime.

Day after day,
Don't want to listen to the stupid words they say.
They say they bully,
But they don't know me.

Then walk off saying why can't we get on?
Where are they coming from?

People Need To Learn How To Do Tame

Cambridge is my home,
I used to think of them as my people.
But what they have been doing is truly evil,
They are not tame and untame people.

Taming has spread like a disease,
It's enough to bring me to my knees.
They have become stupid sick people,
Taming is illegal.

I don't know how many people have been hurt,
These people are dirt.
If you ask why, you just get told it's taming,
It is not entertaining.

I miss how Cambridge was when I was young,
Taming should have never begun.

People Used To Say Good Morning

People used to say good morning,
But I guess that's boring.
Now they say, "keep tame,"
It's so lame.

There is something wrong with the people of Cambridge,
It's like they don't understand language.
The untame people can't read and write,
They are not bright.

The people don't care if this is true,
This isn't something people should do.
It is harassment and abuse,
Not just the stupid language they use.

They won't listen to a word I say,
Should not be this way.

Should Not Be This Way

They keep telling me I can't move forward,
It does make me feel awkward.
Everything I do will fail,
I should be in jail.

All I have to do is be peaceful,
This isn't normal.
Is that fact?
It doesn't matter how I react.

It's always who have I hit.
I can't intimidate,
It really does aggravate.
I don't hit people,
Taming is stupid dribble.

They said they will tame me until I'm dead.
All you can do is say we bully,
It's a bit hard not to get angry.

Don't know if they believe what they say,
Should not be this way.
Fuck what they say.

Protect And Serve

Can't believe my own eyes,
They are telling lies.
Dad told me to respect the law,
But I'm not sure anymore.

Dad said don't be on the wrong side,
Go in colour blind.
Never hit anyone on the street in my life,
They go home to their kids and wives.

Do they even care?
This is not fair.

Sick And Dirty

Everywhere I go people ask me who have I hit,
I keep on telling them I don't do it.
They just say I keep on hitting people,
Who are they trying to fool?

Day after day, week after week,
Month after month, year after year.

Or it's have people been hitting me,
These people are so cold and empty.
Then it's I can't read or write, what if I couldn't?
Do they just want an argument?

They say it's because I'm untame,
This is so insane.

They do everything they can to make me feel like shit,
And I've had enough of it.

They keep saying I won't live to 30,
I'm 42,
These people are sick and dirty.

Stupid Immaturity

They just keep on pestering me for my attention,
Telling me to keep tame is such a stupid expression.
Then it's we are breaking your heart, and you will fall apart.

I have never known so much stupid immaturity,
Why do these people even bother talking to me?
You think you are as tough as Manny Pacquiao,
These people can go to hell.

I'm not even a fighter,
I'm trying to be a writer.
Then it's why do people beat you up?
Well they don't,
I've had enough.

Stupid Twats

What they have been doing in Cambridge,
Is more than misuse of language.

Tame does not mean peaceful,
Why talk to me like I'm a fool.
They sound like they never went to school,
I'm not a ghoul.

Why treat me like an animal, this is criminal.
They need to wash the poison out of their brains,
they are so vain.

Need to explain again.
Taming is what they do to big cats,
Sick of them stupid twats.

Tame Time

As the people keep passing me by,
Everything they say is a lie.

Who have you hit?
Why do people hit you?
It doesn't matter how many times I say this is not true.
It's always the same everyday, we need to keep you tame.

Then it's you can't even read or write,
With so much spite.
Then they smile and say it's tame time,
Don't they get this is a terrible crime?

This isn't just stupid street slang,
The people who invented it should hang.
These people sound so uneducated,
It is so sick what they did.

Tame

You are not born mature,
You grow into it or you do not.
Don't you know a lot?
Go with what you got,
You haven't got a shot.
Were you born to be tame?
You are so lame.

Part 2

FINDING HOPE

The sun blazing in the sky,
Walking through town, I wonder why?
A question being asked, no skip to the beat,
As I'm pounding the pavement with my feet.

They look at me with disgust, mirth, pity and horror.
Trying to ignore it, show them I'm not bothered.
But I am, it is so exhausting to pretend.
To drag out this performance to the bitter end.

I'm not hurting anyone,

I'm peaceful, content.
Why do they always goad me,
Looking at me like I'm excrement?

Just need to keep my cool,
Remind myself it's them not me.
I can't change their perceptions,
I'll just let it be.

But then someone will approach me,
Come in for the kill,
Testing my patience, control, and self will.

They'll not trap me like this,
I'm better than that,
I will not dance to their tune,
Nor lash out at the twat.

I will remain focused,
I will remain calm,
I'll ignore the remarks,
And looks of alarm.

Because walking through town on this beautiful day,

Makes life worth living and I'd like to say,
That there are always the haters, those who just can't see,
That I'm bettering myself, being the best version of me.

Finding Hope

Hope is a funny old thing, and your perception of hope changes as your circumstances evolve. There was a time when my hopes were centred around my heart, the love I held for another. I hoped for a life we were building together, for happiness and companionship. I was blinded by this hope, but it was not hope's fault. Hope is the feeling, the road, the journey. When we arrive at the destination we see there is now a new destination, a new hope.

I hoped to find someone I could love, once there I hoped we could become one, and then move in together. My distant hope was marriage and a family. I was traveling down that road before the bridge collapsed and I found that route had disappeared to that particular place with this person.

I veered off road, my new hope getting through the day without having to think too much about her, that journey I had been on which had come to an abrupt end. The road turned into a downhill slope and I followed it deeper into the unknown. I could have stopped at any point and turned around to go back to before my journey with her. I still had my flat, I still had my job, I still had my sanity, but no, I continued down into the Valley of despair, willingly falling into it's depths.

I was depressed. Hope was something I used to have in my life but now I was preoccupied with this new path towards darkness. I didn't care when I lost my job. I didn't care when I lost my flat. I feared nothing. I didn't care.

The path I was on, the journey I was making, had it's own destination, that being death. I believe I would have got there eventually, following that particular road further and further down into the valley. Fortunately there are people in this world who care. People who have travelled the same road you are on and help veer you onto a better route, out of the valley and back into the sun.

The climb up often takes a lot longer than the descent, but the thorns give way to flowers, gravel to grass, the air starts to smell a little sweeter and before you know it, in front of you, in the distance, is hope again.

I'm still climbing, I know. My hopes are different from those of the person I once was, and that's ok. *He* hadn't been through the valley, *he'd* never understand why things have change for me.

I hope the words I write can reach people. My poems are my journal, my way of getting these thoughts out of my head and letting go, not allowing myself to slip downwards and fall back to the valley base. It is self therapy, and that's what I need to battle the demons in my head. If they reach another tortured soul and resonate, that's great, but I write them for myself first and foremost, it is baggage I need to shed so that I can climb out of the valley without it weighing me down.

There are people who wish to trip me up, to see me slide, but I won't let them. When I was at the bottom of my valley I would have lashed out but not anymore. I have other means of defending myself through my words.

There is a word I mention from time to time, and that word is tamed. People want to tame me, to control me, have me conform to their expectations, but these people haven't seen what I've seen and haven't been where I have been. They've never seen the bottom of the valley, been without hope. I will not be tamed, controlled, or conform to their expectations. I will be me, broken but on the mend, untamed, wild, free, and with hope once again.

'Gay boy. Look at you, you little puff,' the Goblin sneers at me.

I'm sat in the lounge area at the shelter, reading the first draft of my short collection of poems, entitled Untamed.

It's funny he should perk up at this moment because I've just finished reading one of my poems entitled *Evil Goblin*. Yes, it's about him.

I smile, looking him dead in the eye and tell him to fuck off, before getting up and leaving the room.

'Yeah, go on,' he calls after me. 'Go back to your wank pit and watch some gay bastard porn.'

I shake my head as I leave, laughing at his pathetic attempt to provoke a reaction from me.

I'm not gay. I don't care if someone is, it's their choice. Live and let live is what I say, but the fact this idiot thinks he can use the idea of my being homosexual as a prop to make me lose my cool is hilarious. It would mean I'd care about something he has spewed out of his rotten mind. I don't. He's not even real to me, the Goblin. He's a caricature, a poem in my book which I can close whenever I like.

'Faggot!' Is his last parting gift as I head down to reception and out into the sun.

Cambridge in June. The embodiment of great British summertime. The sun is out, there's a slight breeze in the air carrying the scent of freshly cut lawns. I love it. On a day like today nothing can stop the hope from shining through.

I'm headed to the pub. On a day like today, what better way to spend it than out in the beer garden with a few mates. There was a time when I relied up those people to help me shut away thoughts of a love and a life lost. They became friends, they became the people I could talk to, a distraction from real life, while themselves teetering upon the edge of the valley themselves.

Yes I still drink. It wasn't the drink's fault. It was my fault. My state of mind back then. I allowed myself to be consumed, to slip down that slope, but now I'm beyond that and it'll be nice to see a few familiar faces. I forced myself to stay away while I got my life together, my head together, and now the reward is revisiting these people and having a laugh, rekindling friendships which I hold dear. I might even pass around my copy of Untamed, see what they think. No doubt I'll have some of them take the piss, but that's fine as well. Good natured banter amongst friends.

Taming Is Evil

When I start my morning walk,
I can dismiss it as just stupid talk.
As time goes by,
All I can do is wonder why they lie.

Is always the same day after day, week after week,
I wonder do these people even think?
It's hard to believe people can be so stupid,
Why do they even do it?

Everyday need to keep me tame, is always the same.
I try to say I'm not a lion I'm a man, really I'm not Tarzan.

But they harass me everywhere I go,
I try to tell them I just don't want to know.
It's always I can't read or write,
I hit people, is not true, taming is evil.

Taming Is Evil 2

Telling people to keep tame sounds like something
from a carry on movie,
It's so goofy.
I've had enough of this cheesy talk,
These people are ruining my walk.

They keep on saying they won't leave me be,
Why do they even want to talk to me?
Everyday always the same, again and again.

Who have you hit?
So sick of this stupid shit.
I'm not Floyd Mayweather,
This is not very clever.

I don't hit people, taming is evil.

Taming Is Evil 3

The people of Cambridge,
Have really dumbed down their language.
It is more than stupid use of language,
Taming has caused so much anguish.

Again and again, I won't live until I'm 40,
They don't even know me.
Wish I was still in my 30's,
These people are so dirty.

They say taming will give me a heart attack,
Not what I would call a wisecrack.
Trying to take me to school, because I hit people.
Is not true, that is something I don't do.

They never think what they are doing is wrong,
This has been going on for far too long.

Taming Is Mad

These stupid sick people,
How did they get so backward and evil?
Had it up to my eyeballs,
They are silly fools.

They keep on saying I can't read or write,
Looking at me like I want to fight.
Need to explain,
People are not tame or untame.

Keep on saying everything I do will fail,
What the hell!
Why can't they understand?
This taming is mad.

Taming Is Terrible

Taming is from the Twilight Zone,
They just make it up as they go.
I try to explain,
Lions and tigers are tame and untame.

They say I'm not a tame man,
Like I'm some kind of bogeyman.
For years they have been saying I hit people,
Treating me like I don't mean a thing at all.

All this time haven't even thrown one punch,
These people don't know much.
But again they say I'm an untame man,
So I try what like Tarzan?

This just isn't funny,
The way they think is dark and muddy.
Taming is terrible,
It doesn't make people peaceful.

Taming Means You're A Nobody

As they walk past,
They don't think fast.
They bully,
Not sure if I understand fully.

I'm just one of the people they bully.
Won't fool me, on't school me.
Everyday we bully who are we?

After all these years,
Drinking so many beers.
Never even thrown one punch,
They don't know much.

These people are sick,
Just so thick.
It's because I'm untame,
Even though they don't know my name.

They keep saying I hit people, this is not playing.

Taming Ruin's Life

Nobody cares if what they are saying is true,
They just don't have a clue.
The people in this town have gone insane,
Man is not tame and untame.

The whole thing is built on a house of lies.
With smiles they say we are breaking your heart.
Their eyes light up, when they ask have you been beaten up.
More like demons than humans, they can all go to hell.

Taming Will Ruin Your Heart

Taming will ruin your heart,
What have these people been doing?
They say all you have to do is be tame,
They accept no blame.

I have never heard so many sick stupid words,
Whatever I say is not heard.
Tame does not mean peaceful,
These people are bloody awful.

They just won't learn,
Makes me want to leave and never return.

Taming Will Tear You Apart

Taming will tear you apart,
    And break your heart.
    Then it's everything I do will fail,
    These people can go to hell.

Can't even do who will I meet,
    That's what they say when they pass me on the street.
    Have people been hitting you?
    Or who have I hit, this is stupid shit.

They are so fake.

Wish Cambridge could be swallowed up by a big earthquake.

Telling Lies

They treat me like I'm a character on a T.V. show,
And they are making a cameo.
Standing in queue, don't even know you.
Telling me to be tame, over and over again.

Saying I hit people,
And people hit me.
Saying I can't read or write,
These people are not very bright.

Telling me I won't live to be 40,
Well I'm 42 so fuck you.
Won't give me a key,
Don't even know me.

Don't the people know what they are doing is wrong?
Won't make me feel like I don't belong.
They said they will tame me until I'm dead,
Need to wash that poison out of your head.

Terrible Crime

How can the people of Cambridge use such backward language?
Keep tame, keep tame, again and again.

It's so bloody stupid, they don't care how I'm affected.
They say they know what I do, but when I ask they just don't have a clue.

Then it's why do people beat you up?
How many people have you hit?

It's not true, this is not what people should do.
They don't even know my name.

This has been going on for such a long time,
Taming is a terrible crime.

Them Stupid Ugly Teachers

Been going on for such a long time,
Glad they are not children of mine.
They just keep telling lies,
Seen it with my own eyes.

People are not tame and untame,
They do more than complain.
Causing me problems with people on the street,
It feels like it's with everyone I meet.

They keep on saying I hit people,
Them teachers are evil.
Keep on saying I can't read or write,
They are more than just impolite.

Should not teach it in schools,
Them teachers are fools.

There Is No Such Thing As An Untame Man

These people are just bloody awful,
There are not tame and untame people.
Taming is harassment and abuse,
I'm so sick of the stupid language they use.

Can keep on saying I can't read or write,
I'm just gonna think you're not very bright.
How could this happen in Cambridge?
It's more than stupid use of language.

Can keep on saying you're breaking my heart,
I'm just gonna think you're not very smart.
This needs to end.
It is driving me around the bend.

This Has Gone Too Far

People are not tame or untame.

They don't even do that with feral children,
These sick people, I will never forgive them.
Everyday it's I hit people and I can't read or write,
They do it all day long and at night.

I have lost my faith in humanity,
These people don't even know me.
They are so shallow and cold,
I get it from children and the old.

I don't know how many untame people there are,
But this has gone way too far.

They just say we call it taming,
This needs explaining.

They teach it in church,
They teach it in schools,
The people of Cambridge of are sick fools.

Too Much Ill Will

Never know so much crazy bullshit,
I've had enough of it.
These people don't care about the words they say.
Don't ever think they are doing things the
wrong way.

Do I really need to say it again?
People are not tame or untame.
Do the people know what has been going on?
They can't feel a thing, just keep lying.

We Are Driving You Crazy

Everyday listening to the sick words.
We are breaking your heart, pretending I'm going to start.

They won't listen to a word I say,
It should not be this way.
I need to explain people are not tame or untame.
Why do I need to explain?
This is insane.

Had it up to the eyeballs
To hell with them sick fools.

Voodoo

As I walk away,
Don't want to listen to the words they say.
They refuse to leave me be,
And say I won't get a key.

Even as I walk away,
They just keep saying I'm untame.

Old women on the street,
People in shops,
People working on roof tops.
It's the same everyday,
I need to keep tame.

I don't know how many people they do this to,

Some say it is like voodoo.
It's always who have I hit,
Not sure if they mean it.

Don't know how many people have been beaten up.
I have had enough.
They just keep on lying,
They would be happy if I was crying.

What Side?

They were on my side,
Now they are just taking me for a ride.
People on the street,
Could kick me with their feet.

Can punch my head in,
Will give them a ring.
But people keep saying this not playing.

I'm the one that hits people,
This is evil.
It just isn't true,
What can I do?

They talk to me like I'm a moron,
And I don't belong.

Why Can't We Get On?

They keep saying I can't read or write,
With so much spite.
Then it's have people been hitting me,
What con can they see?

Keep telling me everything I do will fail,
And I should be in jail.
Then walk off saying why can't we get on,
Trying to make me feel like I don't belong.

Don't know why they only do this to the poor,
Can't take anymore.
They don't care if it's a lie,
Asking me if I want to cry.

People are not tame or untame,
They never think they are doing it the wrong way.

Why Do They Lie?

I need to be kept from hitting people,
Talking to me like I'm evil.
Can't understand,
This is mad.

Been doing this everyday,
Saying I need to be kept tame.
They say I won't live until I'm 40,
I'm 42, none of what they say is true.

Keep saying it's destroying my heart,
These people are not very smart.
Everybody all of the time,
Don't know why they lie.

Then it's I can't read or write,
Don't want any of these people in my life.

Won't Leave Me Be

Looking into the eyes of some stupid sad old man.
Just some lame brain, telling me to be tame.

They say I'm unemployable, why don't go out on the pull?
Should put me in a cell, all of these people can go to hell.

They harass me all of the time, I feel like I'm going out of my mind.
Everyday it's who have I hit? Do they even believe it?

Day after day, such ugly spiteful words they say.

I really miss going to the library, they keep lying about me.

I don't know how many people they have done this to,
This is not what people should do.

You Just Keep On Hitting People

Not the American Cambridge,
If they can understand the language.

Tame does not mean peace,
Will this ever cease?

They just can't learn,
They want to see me burn.

Don't know how it is for the other untame people,
They sound so feeble.

As they pass me by,
It's enough to make me cry.

Keep saying I hit people,
I just keep on hitting people.

Will They Ever Leave Me Alone?

Walking down the street,
Can't even count to three,
Before they harass me.

They say it is because I hit people,
It's a bit hard to keep my cool.
I tell them that the police know it's not true,
But they just say we know you do.

All you do is watch T.V.,
It's obvious they haven't got a clue about me.
Perhaps they watch too much T.V.
Why be that way with me?

We call it taming,

It is a bit samey.
Then it's you can't read or write,
They do it with no contrite.

These people have got so sick,
The way they talk is so thick.
Will they ever leave me alone?
So glad none of them are there when I get home.

On My Own

They are boring my brains out,
Don't want them about.
Everyday don't want to listen to what they say say,
Don't want to play.

I do ask them why they won't leave me be,
What can they see?
They think I'm somebody else,
I sometimes wonder why I try.

In shops, on roof tops, on the street,
There isn't anyone I want to meet.
I like being on my own,
Don't even want anyone to phone.

Numpty

They say I need to be tamed,
What next? Need to be house trained?
They ask me if I know Humpty Dumpty,
Like I'm a numpty.

I try to look them in the eyes,
And ask do you want to traumatise?
Are you trying to hypnotise?
Why keep telling lies?

I did not grow up in a zoo,
They don't have a clue.

Book 3 in The Untamed Series

The Man Among the Stones

I stink.

I can smell the two weeks of body odour, feel the grime glistening on my skin from beneath the layers I wear to off the the cold.

Each evening, as the city lights dim and a quiet creeps in behind the wind, I climb the hill away from the city centre and head for the cemetery. No one ever bothers me there. The dead, it would seem, are good roommates, quiet, undemanding, and generous with space.

Tonight is a reasonably warm night, but the temperature will drop. It is forecast rain in the early hours so it would be best to make camp in the church doorway so that I'm not sodden by the morning. A shame really, because I'd have liked to drift off in my favorite spot in the graveyard, the wide stone bench situated between two weathered tombs of forgotten families. From there I can see most of the city, the rooftops glowing like embers under the night sky. When rain isn't forecast I will roll out my old sleeping bag (which spends its days hidden in the bushes close by), and tuck my jacket under my head, listening to the gentle rustling of leaves and distant hum of traffic as I'm carried off to sleep.

I didn't always sleep in a graveyard, and from an outsider's view it might even appear quite macabre, but it beats trying to bunk down in the city, where the forever fluorescent hue of the night and the chances of being robbed and beaten by other street dwellers, is never far away.

Things weren't always like this.

I had a job, friends, hopes, dreams, a life I was heading towards, a woman who liked me, a women who was my everything. Circumstance can often flip itself on it's head though. My job had been a kitchen porter at a local hotel, no great position but the work was continuous throughout the year and the position came with staff accommodation. A room of my own, double bed, desk, wardrobe, ensuite bathroom with power-shower, my little haven.

The first one to disappear was the girl. It always is. There had been no blazing row, no violence, no inkling that we weren't happy. One day I simply received a text message saying it wasn't working out, that I'm a great guy but I'm not what she wants at this stage in her life. The classic *"It's me not you"* used throughout the ages of breakups. And that was that. Heart broken, I reached out to my friends for support without even realizing that as a couple we had shared friends. Her friends. A couple of her girlfriend's partners took me out a beer, one last hurrah before melting into obscurity and casting me out of the clique.

What does one do when finding themselves alone with no support? I started drinking. First it was in the pubs in the city, wanting to bit of company, even if that company was of strangers. Sometimes I'd start chatting to groups, one time I even took a woman home at the end of the night, but drinking out every night gets expensive and so I'd start buying in. My little room in the hotel became a prison of despair fueled by alcohol induced hopelessness.

Then it happened.

I was called into the supervisor's office one morning and told there had been a few complaints about me appearing drunk on shift. I explained that was never the case, although there might have been occasions where I'd been drinking the previous night and was perhaps not the freshest the next morning. We agreed I'd try and curb my evening activities when working the next day, but that only sent me further down the rabbit hole. Knowing my work mates were now distancing themselves from me too, drove me to drink more.

I was so alone.

It wasn't long before I was reprimanded by work, and then in no time was told, *"We're afraid we're going to have to let you go."*

Where do you go when there's nowhere to go?

Nowhere.

A victim of circumstance, riding the wave of depression right down, literally into the gutter, onto the streets. You are now not living, you're simply existing, and that existence is survival. Civilized society is stripped away from you and now your evolution has rewound. You are an animal wearing a man's mask wondering how it came to this.

The money I had soon went, spent first on trying to find a new job with accommodation quickly during the day, and drinking myself into oblivion so that I'd pass out for a few glorious hours and not feel the bite of the elements at night.

Why didn't I reach out to my family?

My mother and father lived abroad. They weren't just around the corner so that I could go "home" so to speak, lie in my childhood bed and start again. It was more than that though. It was not wanting to admit to my family that I had failed. Some misguided sense of pride is what kept me on the streets at first. After a while though I was just here.

I remember one night. I must have been living rough for a month or so at the time.

It was a Friday evening and I had been drinking in the park all day. It had been sunny and as strange as this might sound, sunny days could make you feel free. Free of the glances from embarrassed passer-byers as you ask if they could spare any change, free of judgment because you are just one of many chilling out in the sun on a nice day.

I had been drinking with a couple of Polish guys I knew from the streets, basking in the glorious Cambridge summertime. I had eight cans of strong lager for the park and a bottle of Jack Daniels for later on when the temperature dropped.

By early afternoon a was pissed.

The Polish guys were sharing their own beers with me on top of the strong lager I'd been drinking. The Jack Daniels was opened and by the evening I could hardly stand.

Staggering through town, back towards the church and my bench amongst the dead, I heard someone call out from across the road.

'Errr, Nigel!'

I couldn't see.

Drunken tunnel vision and my need to get back drove me on.

'Nigel,' again.

From across the road I saw people waving, and in my zombie-like state lurched over to them.

'Fucking hell mate, you alright?' One of them sniggered. My once friends, out on a night out with their ladies and…there she was. My lady. My girl. The one who claimed it was her and not me and that is why she had to leave, to ghost me, to cease from existence when I thought we had our lives to share.

Feigning concern, she approached, a new face within the cackle of once friends, emerged by her shoulder, his hand reaching down to brush past hers.

The new guy. Of course.

'Are you ok?' She asked.

I tried to speak, to say something witty and self-depreciating, something to have her think what she saw in front of her wasn't me. I recall sounds escaping my throat, drivel. Pissed up uttering from a tramp who was heading back to his bench while the person who started off this chain reaction had found her replacement and was still living a real life.

Behind her one of the group said, 'Still hammering the booze I see,' smiling, giggling, ridiculing me.

Had my drinking been a running joke while we'd been together? One whispered whenever I was out of earshot?

I never drank anymore than they did. We'd go out to pubs and clubs and we'd have a good time as a group of friends and lovers. That comment stuck with me though, as I shook my head and continued on my way, ignoring her calls back to me. Had I been a running joke? Had I drunk a little more than them? Been a little more pissed than them? And was this the reason she had broken up with me? Peer pressure, succumbing to the one sided argument that I wasn't right for her without ever broaching the subject with me?

That comment was a catalyst.

Fuck her and fuck her mates.

I would get off the streets. I would find myself a place not conditioned to the whims of an employment contract, and if I ever saw any of them again I would just smile. They are worth no more of my time than that.

You know it's amazing what opportunities can be found through positive thinking. Not a week had passed since that encounter that I was approached by the homeless shelter and asked if I'd like to do some volunteering.

I grasped this with both hands, helping at the shelter and then moving on to cleaning the church whose doorways had helped fend off the coldest of nights. Hot tea and biscuits every morning, and free cinema tickets on occasions, allowing me to lose myself for a few hours a couple of times a week.

From there I was able to get myself into a shared housing project and once again felt the luxury of a mattress underneath me as I slept. I didn't stop drinking, not right away. Alcohol can help. It can help you socialize with others who have had a hard time and are trying, trying to find a way back into society. Alcohol can also help dampen the hard times.

I came back from the brink and the irony that the reason behind my downfall was also the push I needed to get me off the streets, is not lost on me. All I needed was a little fuck you motivation and to see from outside eyes, through their eyes, what I had become.

I haven't yet seen them out and about, but that smile is ready.

I'm not the person they though of me, and I'm still on my way up.

The Big Jizz

'Hey, you boy. You got that money I lent you?'

His rancid breath stale with cigarettes and cheap cider, almost has me gagging.

Do I have his money?

Is this guy for real?

Is he joking?

'What money?' I ask, careful to veer out of the way of his next exhale of breath as he opens his mouth.

'Listen boy, you know what money. You owe me £40. I lend it you, I want it back.'

I stare vacantly at this idiot.

Big Jizz, he calls himself.

A big pile of jizz if you ask me. The remnants

of so many possibilities if only evolution had tried a little harder. Swaying in the urine stained doorway, he smiles at me, the yellowed teeth peeling through his slightly parted lips.

What a loser.

One of life's fuck ups.

And a wannabe gangster who appears to forget things inconvenient to him. Like, for instance, the fact that it is I who lent him money to the tune of £200. It wasn't all at once. I didn't just throw notes in his face and tell him it's fine, pay me back when you can. No. Big Jizz asked to borrow a tenner. I was happy to lend it him. I'm not without money and so because he promised to give it me back the following week, I felt I wouldn't miss it.

When payday was upon Big Jizz, he was nowhere to be seen. A creature of habit, roaming the same streets day in and day out, had vanished, or at least made sure our paths didn't cross.

Then when I did see him he was so, so sorry. He'd messed his money up and would I be able to lend him another thirty and he'd give me fifty back the next day.

Apprehensive, I felt I couldn't say no. I wanted my money back, even something as small as ten pounds. It was the principle. And so, yes, I lent him a further thirty.

This is what they do you see, these wannabe gangsters. They lie and they cheat people and then smile to your face and act as though you're still friends, buddies, compadres when in reality they're just laughing at you behind your back.

'Next week?' I asked, 'I'll get fifty pounds back from the forty I've now lent you.'

'No worries my man, of course.'

Two days later Big Jizz came to me with an opportunity. He was going to buy some weed and sell it on, making himself a tidy profit and I would then get my money back.

'Maybe you want to lend me a little more and you can come in on the profits from the weed?'

My initial reaction was to say no, tell him to fuck off, that all I wanted was the fifty pounds he now owed me, but greed is a powerful emotion.

'How much do you need?'

The Big Jizz shrugged, 'Another hundred? You know I'm good for it, we'll make a lot of money from this.'

'How much money? Because you'll owe me £150.'

Another smile.

More bile breath.

'Can you afford to make it to £200 in total, my man? A nice round number and you'll see it double.'

'Double?' I said. 'So I'll get £400 back?'

'Guaranteed.'

I considered this.

Like I said, I had money. I had saved a decent chunk, my rainy day fund. My means of leaving this town if ever I wanted to. A safety net which would mean I could start again somewhere new.

'£400?'

That snake's smile again.

I agreed to his terms.

'How long will I have to wait to get my money?' I asked.

Big Jizz shrugged, 'couple of days maybe. Don't worry bro, this legit, yeah?'

I smile, looking the man up and down. Legit is perhaps the one word I wouldn't use to describe Big Jizz's activities. Nor his appearance or overall personality. Ducking and diving from people, always attempting to intimidate others. This man was an idiot. A wannabe gangster who was now getting into low-level drug dealing funded by me. I was already beginning to regret engaging with him at all.

£200 turned into £400 did sound appealing though. I agreed and Big Jizz was nice enough to escort me to the cash machine and watch me withdraw the funds.

'Can never be too careful around these parts,' he said, standing as my sentry by the side of the hole in the wall. The irony was not lost on me. That *he* would be saying you can never be too careful when it was the likes of the Big Jizz from whom you needed to be careful around.

I handed over the notes.

'When will I see my money back?'

'Soon bro, soon as I done this, yo.'

I nodded. I needed a beer. Preferably somewhere void of the Jizz. Despite me handing over the cash, he'd be happy to follow me around all day trying to score free drinks from me. No thanks, not today.

'A week?' I asked.

Another smile, 'yeah, yeah, a week. You'll have your dough back then.'

I walked away and didn't see him for two months.

. . .

'Hey, you boy. You got that money I lent you?'

'What money?' I say.

'Listen boy, you know what money. You owe me £40. I lend it you, I want it back.'

He did give me £40. Three weeks after I handed him over my £200 I happened to see him one day and went mad at him. Where the fuck was my £400?

'It's coming bro, soon.'

'I want it back. You're taking the piss.'

'No can do. Business is in motion.'

Eventually he agreed to a 10% down payment. £40. Now apparently he "lent" me that £40 while owing me £400.

'So what the fuck you talking about, I owe you £40. You owe me £360, you dickhead,' I shouted at him.

'Yo yo, bro,' he said, getting up in my face, 'don't be calling me no dickhead. Are you real? I'll see you buried boy.'

Buried? Really? This streak of piss couldn't lift a fucking shovel, never mind dig a hole to bury me in. Good luck with that.

'I want my money.'

'Carries on and you'll get nothing.'

This guy.

It wasn't even about the money. I didn't really care if I saw the phantom £400 or if I just got my £200 back. It was the fact he's so blatantly stringing me along and I was foolish enough to go along with it. Shame on me. Shame on me for ever trusting low life scum.

'You think you can intimidate me by asking me for £40 when you owe me a lot more?'

'Actually, no bro. I'm a business man, yeah? I lend you £40 and now you owe me £60. Call it interest for disrespecting me.'

The red veil descended.

I'm nobody's mug.

I swung my fist hard and fast, making bone crunching contact with his nose.

The Big Jizz crumpled to the floor. While down there I put a couple of boots in, screaming, 'give me my fucking money. Disrespect you!'

I lent down and put my hand in his jacket pocket. A roll of notes. Got to be a grand there easy.

'What the fuck is this?' I asked.

'You leave that, that someone else's. You'd be a brave boy taking their bank.'

I smiled, unrolling the notes and counting out 18 20 pound notes. I was going to just take my initial investment back but fuck it, why should scumbags profit while pissing on the rest of us.

Dropping the rest of the money like confetti on top of him, I put another boot in and walked away. Next time I'll remind myself that if something appears too good to be true…it usually is.

Blood and Money

Going to war,
Want to get paid some more.
So Sick of being poor,
Training is a chore.
I wonder what I'm doing it for.

Then it's as if I was never there,
Does anyone even care?
I've got to get up again,
We are only men.

It meant so much,
Now I sound like I'm speaking double dutch.
I gave it everything I had,
At least the weather wasn't bad.

I now I need a normal job,
No longer ruled by the mob.
Getting up for a brand new day,
We can't all be Sugar Ray.

Fear

Can you lie your way out of it?
Can you fight your way out of it?
Tell them you don't give a shit.

You need backup,
Put your hands up.
I will tell you one more time,
That's mine.

Who do you think you are?
Living in a T.V dreamworld,
You're someone in the underworld.

Moody

Going to get proper moody,
You little cutie.
Going to knock your head off,
Don't you dare run off.

Going to beat the stupid,
Out of you.
You don't have a clue.
What will you do?

Poncy Queen

Do you want it to be unseen?
You are not very clean.
Can't talk to me that way.
Don't want to stay.

Need to go to bed,
Wish you were dead.
Get your eyeball off,
Do you need to cough?

Will go hell,
Should be in a cell.

People should keep tame

Not Listening

Pretending you can't hear me.
Why are you free?
What a stupid game.
What is your name?

Where are you from?
You are in the wrong.
Why can't you do your job properly?
You don't know me.

The Worst

The worst weirdo.
Mellow Yellow, we know.

What an ugly, stupid man.
Should be in a cell, will go to hell.

Makes me want to puke my guts up,
Want to say, put your hands up.

Will be here tomorrow.
Can you follow?

One more thing to say,
You hate me everyday.

Stupid people

Them stupid little people.
Can knock you down,
And treat you like a clown.
Going to kick you in the teeth,
Going to give you some more grief.
Will knock your head off,
Don't try to run off.
Going to tear you apart.
And your'e not very smart.

Void

Can't fill the void.
I feel so annoyed.
Wish it was like years ago.
Family and friends,

Dad said, 'It'll all change.'
Mum said, 'You should wed.'
I've had enough,
I just want my bed.

Up for a new day,
There's people I need to pay,
Words I need to say.

Feel my life isn't real,
I need to heal.
When you were there,
You know I care.

My life I want to share.

Lunatic

That lunatic is well thick.
He needs a kick.
Could throw a brick?
Is it just taking the mick?

That savage can not manage.
They call him untamed,
A rather odd name.
He has been going insane, again.

Can't Sleep

I can try counting sheep,
But I just can't get,
Any sleep.

Gob

Will hurt his heart,
And damage his soul.
Will be a home goal.
I will beat him down,
Make him frown.
Will fail,
And fail,
And fail.
Lose your temper,
Can you remember?
From January to December.
Are you ever gonna act your age?
They should put you in a cage.
Get a job,

Give it some more,
Of your stupid gob.

Taming Is Harassment

Don't you come anywhere near.
Am I being clear?
Don't even eyeball me you fool,
Or I'll take all of you to school,
You tool.
I'm not a lion, what are you on?

Won't Leave Me Be

They come softly creepy,
While I'm still sleepy.
What do they want with me?
Eyeballing and fooling.
I'll listen again,
Need to be tamed.
What did I do wrong?
Who will not belong?
Why not just leave me be?
You are not with me.

Keep Tame

Don't even know my name,
What is, "keeping tame"?
What a load of shit,
Then it's,
"Come on give me a hit."
But you are so old.
Have I got to do what I'm told?

Don't Want Home

I can skip,
I can swim,
Never feel like,
I'm going to win.
It is a sin,
Where have you been?

If you were there,
I'd know life's unfair.
I don't want home,
Want to be on my own.

Where were you?
Where did you go?

NIGEL EDWARDS

Let me know,
Do we all owe?

Get Them All In

What goes around comes around.
Lost and found.
Waiting to hear some sound.
Don't want any of them around.

Want to be on my own,
While I'm at home.
Give me a phone call,
I've been talking to a brick wall.

I need a pen friend,
When will this end?

Chained Melody

You need to hide,
Beyond that great divide.

Whipping me with that chain,
You have no brain.
A dirty thief, you're insane,
The one I blame.

It's funny when you sing and dance,
Lost in your ever consuming trace.
Do you even think?
Do you need a drink?

Are you a fun loving prankster,

Masquerading as a high level gangster?
You should be in a cell,
On your slow walk into hell.

Everyday

Haven't found what I'm looking for,
Want more.
Wish you were in my life,
Even wish you were my wife.

I think about you every day.
I need you to know this is true.
Do you love m too?

Maybe she doesn't care.
Mum told me life's unfair.
And I feel like,
I'm not going anywhere.

Scumbag

You're a scumbag.
Going to use your body,
Like a punchbag.
Again, again, and again.

Tell them you don't give a shit.
Do people just want to have a laugh?
You stink and need a bath.

Do you need to go on the run?
Are you trying to have fun?
Have you been getting high?

Are you short of a few bob?
Why don't you get a job?

Don't Want Home 2

Not sure what I'm doing this for.
Don't want home, feeling so alone.

This isn't a game I want to play.
Don't want to stay.

Might want another coffee.
I Really hope you love me.

One more thing I say,
Love you everyday.

Wish it could be,
That's the last word from me.

Miss Bliss

Hello we all know,
Don't need to bow.
Can go fast and slow.
Are you someone,
I want to know.

See you walking past,
Please don't leave fast.
The question I want to ask.
The words I want to say…
Please stay.

Cry

I did try,
Don't want to make you cry.
You are not that smart,
And yet you're breaking my heart.

Everyday, I always want you to stay.
Everyday, you're the most important thing in the world.

Won't you ever learn?
Not doing this to earn.
I don't want to see,
Your ashes in an urn.

Villain

You are such a villain.
Going to kill him.
Going to beat the shit,
Out of all of them.

Fuck all of them!

Please Stay

Can't take anymore,
Don't care if I'm poor.
So sick of being alone,
On my own, going home.

Walking down the street,
Got some people to meet.
I know she won't be there.
I know she doesn't care.

Don't know how to fix
My broken heart.
Maybe I'm just
Not that smart.

Maybe she'll pop around,
For a cup of tea.
Can't keep hoping,
She wants to see me.

Don't know what to do today.
I just want her to stay.

Walking Around

You don't give a shit,
And you could get hit.
Who do you think you are?
You won't go very far.

I don't know who you are,
Get in the car.
You have gone too far,
Do you think you're a star?

You little lightweight,
You do it with so much hate.
You won't tell the truth,
Do they have proof?

You will go to hell.
You won't see the final bell.

Once Upon a Time In Cambridge

Was it a crime?
Was it mine?
Do you think that this,
Is a pantomime?

Why do you need the money?
You are not funny.
Go and get your crew,
Can do.

You are going to crash,
And hit a brick wall.
You are a fool.
Will take you to school.

Hiding In Church

Talking to me like I'm a boy,
Want to play with a toy?
What are you about?
Want you to leave it out.
What is "keeping tame?"
A rather odd way to complain.

Dog Burglar

Just waiting around.
Homebound.
Need a different colour,
Don't love her.

Need a syringe?
Have you been on a binge?
Want to smoke some more?
Do you wonder why you're poor?

I can shoplift,
Give you a gift.
Just want to have a laugh,
And you need a bath.

I can see in your eyes,
Telling too many lies.
Do you only think about yourself?
You're as small as an elf.

Judeo-Christian

Will you listen?
You sicken.
So it's keep tame,
Well you do the same.

You scaredy cat,
Should not do that.
You are not proper,
Are you a window shopper?

Need to learn,
I'm not a cat.

Little Cloud

Soft as marshmallow,
Proper yellow.
I'll tell him where to go,
He's not someone I know.

Can't wait all day,
Don't want you to stay.
You said that the wrong way,
Don't you know what to say?

Are you looking for some party time?
Is that one mine?
Knock off that stupid act,
Are you trying to get jacked?

Have you ever read a book?
You don't have a good look.
Are you waiting for home?
Will you be on your own?

You lonely little cloud,
You didn't speak very loud.
Am I not allowed?
You will get lost in the crowd.

Waiting

Been waiting for such a long time,
Wish you were mine.
Want to ask you,
Want to be clear.
We can just walk,
We don't need to talk.
On my own again,
I just feel the same.
If I see you again,
I won't cause you pain.
Perhaps tomorrow,
You will know.

Ugly Dirty Thief

Might throw a punch,
Want to throw up my lunch.
Why don't you bed for money?
You are not funny.

You stupid dirty smelly thief,
Go and watch telly.
Trying to lie your way out of it,
You little shit.

Who are you?
Need your crew?
What did you do?

The Woman I Love

It has been such a long time,
Since I was yours and you were mine.
I still miss you every single day,
It can't be any other way.

Echos around in my head,
Every word you said.
I don't know what to do with my time,
Can have some lemon and lime,

I'm trying to live my life,
It's crushing without my wife.
Is there light at the end of this tunnel?
I feel like I don't mean a thing at all.

Super Special

Got a dark sense of humour,
You are supes.
Super special, what the hell?
You could live in a cell,
When I hear a bell.
Not sure what for.
When I come back around,
Need sound.
What have you found?

Falling Apart

You are not very smart,
You silly fart.
You don't have a good look,
Have you ever read a book?

You are falling apart,
We will break your heart.
Who do you think you're fooling?
You need schooling.

Don't Like The Cold

You dirty little creep,
I'm trying to sleep.

What do you mean,
come on then give me a hit?
Fight with me,
Let me see.

But you're so old,
And not very bold.
Soft as a marshmallow yellow.

You make me feel sick,
And you're so thick.

Fatima

You are how far?
Can fly?
Need a reason why.
Don't want you to cry.

Don't want to lie.
Don't want to fly.
Give me a bell,
If I fell.

Donna

Don't want the hocus-pocus,
It will make me lose focus.
I can't talk to God,
I might want chips and cod.

He is never there,
He is where?
I've got to do this on my own,
I don't want home.

Why couldn't I stay?
Was I really in the way?
I'll love you everyday.

If I can remember your name,

Do you feel the same?

Dad said I need to go to bed.
Mum said, soon we'll all be dead.
I want to live in the same home.
Don't want to be on my own.

Door

Don't want to think,
Just want to drink.
Going to quit smoking…
Are you joking?

Got to wait for tomorrow,
Is not what I want to borrow.
I just don't want to know,
Not what I owe.

Been here all day,
And I can pay.
Will listen to what you say,
Did you want to play?

I don't care what you say,
You need to leave today.
Open the door,
Or you'll be on the floor.

Want some more?
What for?
Is it because you're poor?
Go get some more.

Wrong Path

You got it backwards,
You are not winning awards.
You are not who you say you are,
You will not go very far.

Keep waking down the wrong path.
Are we all just having a laugh?
Deep within your eyes,
There is nothing but lies.

Looking for a fight?
Did you ever think I might?
It don't belong to you.
You don't have a clue.

That is not what you should do.

Copyright © 2025 Nigel Edwards 2025
The right of Nigel Edwards to be identified as the author of this work has been asserted by him in accordance with the Copyright, Designs and Patents Act 1988.
All rights reserved. No part of this publication may be reproduced, stored in or introduced into a retrieval system, or transmitted, in any form, or by any means (electronic, mechanical, photocopying, recording or otherwise) without the prior written permission of the publisher. Any person who does any unauthorized act in relation to this publication may be liable to criminal prosecution and civil claims for damages.

Published By Broken Hearted Publishing

Printed in Dunstable, United Kingdom